Splish Splash

# Splish Splash

poems by
**Joan Bransfield Graham**

illustrated by
**Steve Scott**

**Houghton Mifflin Company**
**Boston**

www.houghtonmifflinbooks.com

*Library of Congress Cataloging-in-Publication Data*

Graham, Joan Bransfield.
Splish splash / by Joan Bransfield Graham ; illustrated by Steve Scott.
p. cm.
Summary: A collection of poems celebrating water in its various forms,
from ice cubes to the ocean.
RNF ISBN 0-395-70128-7   PAP ISBN 0-618-11123-9
[1. Water — Juvenile poetry.  2. Children's poetry, American. [1. Water — Poetry.
2. American poetry.] I. Scott, Steve, ill.  II. Title.
PS3557.R213S66 1994  94-1237
811'.54—dc20  CIP  AC

Manufactured in China
SCP  10

With love and thanks always
to my parents,
Dorothy and Carroll Bransfield,
who gave me an ocean,
and to Jim,
Heather, and Aimee,
adventurous sailors all

*J.B.G.*

With love to my parents,
Jean and Bill Scott,
who gave me the encouragement,
and to David Saylor,
who gave me the opportunity

*S.S.*

# WATER

Water is a magic potion,
  it can fill a glass, an ocean,
raging river, tiny tear,
  drops of dew that disappear.
Water often spells surprises
  with its changing forms and sizes,
rain and snow, ponds and brooks,
  water has so many looks,
sounds and moods and colors—yet
  in every shape, it's always WET!

# CLOUDS

Up in the air, a gathering
of water drops, a crowd,
a huddling, a puddling,
just dampness is allowed

from lakes and ponds, many places—
too many to keep track—
but when it rains and rains and pours,
clouds

p u t t h e w a t e r b a c k !

# OCEAN

A wave sneaks up to snatch my toes

then turns around and back it goes

Next a splash to wet my legs . . .

"Come out, come out," each breaker begs.

Push and pull, "Okay, you win!" Skip, flop,

PLOP! Now I'm ALL in!

# CROCODILE TEARS

Oh, crocodile poor crocodillo
cried so hard you soaked your pillow

kept it up for such a while

that's how we got  the r i v e r

# WATERFALL

a water-
     fall
is very
     tall
it starts
     out
at the
     top
it falls
     and
falls and
     falls
and falls
     until
it has to
     STOP
and then it
     does

a kind of HOP a CRASH a SMASH

a giant SPLASH!

# !SPRINKLER!

Don't simmer in the summer

slip into the shade

shimmy

through the sprinkler

sipping lemonade

wiggler

under wavy water

giggle in the sun

summer is

a special time!

for shady wadey fun!

COOLCOOLCOOLCOOLCOOL!

# ICE CUBES

ice cubes
clicking
clatter
clink

crazily
inside
my drink

crystal
chorus
clear
and bold

chattering
about
the cold

# POPSICLE

popsicle
popsicle
tickle
tongue fun
licksicle
sticksicle
please
don't run
dripsicle
slipsicle
melt, melt
tricky
stopsicle
plopsicle
hand all
sticky

# RAIN

rain
has washed
the world today
the green's
a greener
GREEN

the
under- and
the outerwear
and all that's in
between is in-
side out-
side

CLEAN!

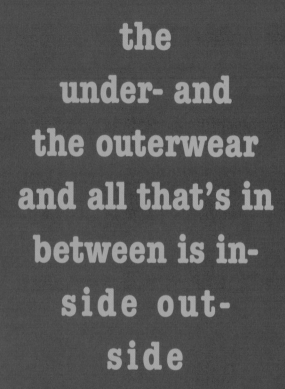

# BABBLING BROOK

babble
banter
burble
blab
prattle
tattle
gossip
gab
mutter
murmur
mumble
hey
please
speak up
what
did
you
say?

# POOL

A pool is full of
cool green shimmer
an invitation for
a swimmer,
it just sits there
plain and flat until
I jump or dive in—
SPLAT! Then I can
feel slippery free,
be anything
I want to be—a seal,
a fish, a bobbing boat,
or just roll on my
back and float.

# HAIL

a
rain
of
ice
such
tiny
balls

that
ping
and
pong
upon
the
w a l l s

that
bounce
around
out
on
the
l a w n

but
look
again
and
they're
all
g o n e

# DEW

spark
the
day

drops
of
dew

born
of
night

catch
the
light

# RIVER

River amble
ramble rush
more than ripples
now you push
rumble tumble
rolling roar
building into

more  and  more
I  watch  you
from  a nearby shore
winding finding
forward flow
churning turning
twisting so
I want to follow
where you go . . .

# STEAM

s

s        t

s

t        e        t

e        a        e

a        m        a

m                 m

boil, boiling, bubbling pot
looks like it's sweaty hot
once was water, now is not
cooking is a clever shaper
turned it into water vapor

# LAKE

*What does it take to make a lake?*
*Lapping, slipping, slapping words*
*boating words, floating words*
*swishing, fishing, squishing words*
*wings and feathers up above, fins below,*
*and when the sun sinks down, a glow,*
*and all that rims the lake, a crown,*
*you see reflected upside down*
*in a kind of mirror glass*
*that ripples when the breezes pass*
*so many words it can take,*
*to start to tell about a lake*

# SNOW

how can
stringing
holes
together

snow
is made
of
crystal
laces

full
of frost
and
empty
spaces

SNOWSNOWSNOW
SNOWSNOWSNOWSNOW
SNOWSNOWSNOWSNOWSNOW
SNOWSNOWSNOWSNOWSNOWSN
SNOWSNOWSNOWSNOWSNOWSN

pile up
into
so much
weather?

OWSNOW
OWSNOW

# POND

*In summertime a pond is great* **for jumping into, splashing,** *swimming.*

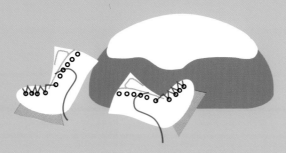

In wintertime
a pond's just right
for *skating over,*
*gliding, skimming.*

Soft with ripples,
hard with ice—
all year long
a pond is nice.

# SHOWER

SHOWER
SHOWER
SHOWER

a shower is
a private cloud
it is a special place
where I can make it
rain so hard
in such a little space

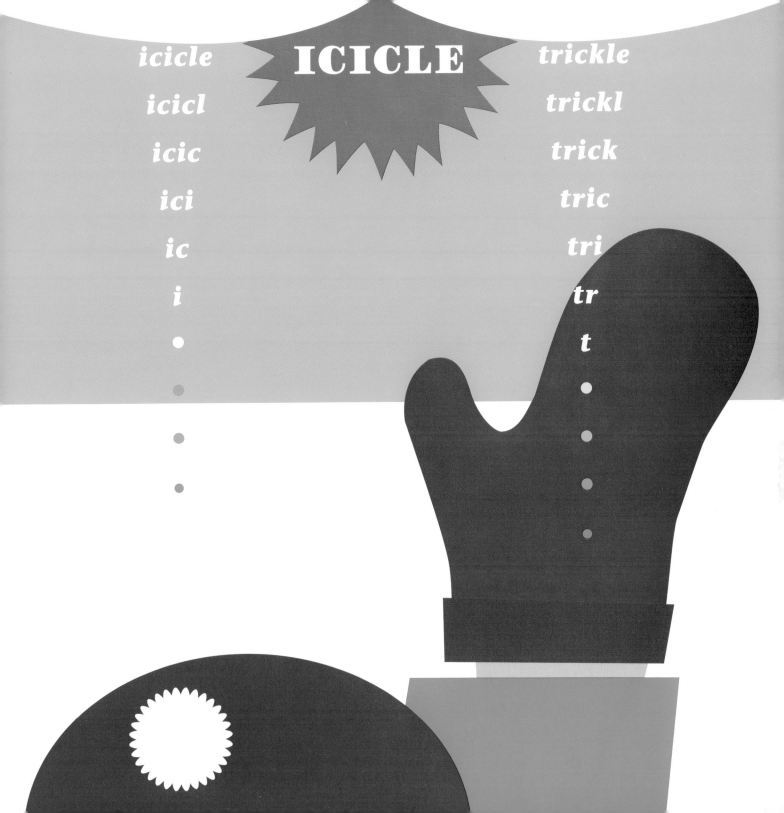

ICICLE

icicle
icicl
icic
ici
ic
i

trickle
trickl
trick
tric
tri
tr
t

# WAVE

Waves gather water building high until they break and wave good-bye